Let's All Sing

...LLECTION FOR YOUNG VOICES
...ured in the Twentieth Century Fox
Television Series GLEE

Original GLEE Arrangements
by Adam Anders and Tim Davis

...apted for publication by Tom Anderson

SO...

MW00980470

TABLE OF CONTENTS

ISBN 978-1-4234-9288-7

HAL•LEONARD®
CORPORATION

7777 W. BLUEMOUND RD. P.O. BOX 13819 MILWAUKEE, WI 53213

Copyright © 2010 by HAL LEONARD CORPORATION
International Copyright Secured   All Rights Reserved

For all works contained herein:
Unauthorized copying, arranging, adapting, recording, Internet posting, public performance,
or other distribution of the printed music in this publication is an infringement of copyright.
Infringers are liable under the law.

Visit Hal Leonard Online at
www.halleonard.com

*Recorded by REO SPEEDWAGON
and Featured in the Twentieth Century Fox Television Series GLEE*

CAN'T FIGHT THIS FEELING

**Original *GLEE* Arrangement
by ADAM ANDERS and TIM DAVIS
Adapted for Publication by TOM ANDERSON**

**Words and Music by
KEVIN CRONIN**

I can't fight_ this feel-in' an - y

long - er,___ and yet I'm still a - fraid_ to let it flow._

___ What start - ed out_ as friend - ship has grown

strong - er,_____ I on-ly wish I had_ the strength to let it show._

___ And e - ven as I wan - der, I'm

keep-in' you_ in sight.___ You're a can-dle in the win - dow_ on a

Copyright © 1984 Fate Music (ASCAP)
This arrangement Copyright © 2010 Fate Music (ASCAP)
International Copyright Secured All Rights Reserved

4

can-dle in the win - dow__ on a cold, dark win-ter's night.___ And

Melody

I'm get - ting clos - er than I___ ev - er thought__ I___ might.__

Harmony

I'm get - ting clos - er than I,_____ Ah__

_____ And I____ can't fight__ this

_____

All **f**

45 *(All)*

feel - in' an - y - more._____ I've for-got-ten what I

start - ed fight - in' for._____ It's time to bring__ this

6

Featured in the Twentieth Century Fox Television Series GLEE

DON'T STOP BELIEVIN'

Original *GLEE* Arrangement
by ADAM ANDERS and TIM DAVIS
Adapted for Publication by TOM ANDERSON

Words and Music by STEVE PERRY,
NEAL SCHON and JONATHAN CAIN

Copyright © 1981 Lacey Boulevard Music (BMI) and Weed-High Nightmare Music (BMI)
This arrangement Copyright © 2009 Lacey Boulevard Music (BMI) and Weed-High Nightmare Music (BMI)
All Rights for Weed-High Nightmare Music Administered by Wixen Music Publishing Inc.
International Copyright Secured   All Rights Reserved

mid-night train_ go - in' an - y - where.___

Dah Dah Dah Dah Dah Dah Dah Dah Dah Dah Dah Dah

18 *opt. Solo 2* *mf*

Just a cit - y boy,_ born and raised in

south De - troit._ He took the mid - night train_ go - in'

end Solo 2 **26** **8**

an - y - where.___

34 *All* *mf*

Some will win,___ some will lose,___ some were born_ to

sing the blues.___ And, oh the mov - ie nev - er ends;_ it goes

42 *opt. Harmony*

on and on_ and on___ and on.___ Stran - gers_

The 1984 #1 Pop Hit by VAN HALEN
and Featured in the Twentieth Century Fox Television Series GLEE

JUMP

Original *GLEE* Arrangement
by ADAM ANDERS and TIM DAVIS
Adapted for Publication by TOM ANDERSON

Words and Music by DAVID LEE ROTH,
EDWARD VAN HALEN, ALEX VAN HALEN
and MICHAEL ANTHONY

Copyright © 1983 Diamond Dave Music, WB Music Corp. and Van Halen Music
This arrangement Copyright © 2010 Diamond Dave Music, WB Music Corp. and Van Halen Music
All Rights for Diamond Dave Music Administered by Red Stripe Plane Music, LLC
All Rights for Van Halen Music Administered by WB Music Corp.
All Rights Reserved   Used by Permission

12

I ain't the worst that you've seen.

Melody

Oh, can't you see what I mean?

Harmony

Ain't the worst that you've seen.

All

Migh's well* jump.

Can't you see what I mean?

42 (All)
shout

Jump! Migh's well jump. Go a-head, jump.

Jump! Go a-head and jump.

50

How old are you? Who said that? Ba-by, how you

been? You say you don't know. You won't

* "Migh's well" = Might as well

14

LEAN ON ME

Original *GLEE* Arrangement
by ADAM ANDERS and TIM DAVIS
Adapted for Publication by TOM ANDERSON

Words and Music by
BILL WITHERS

Copyright © 1972 INTERIOR MUSIC CORP.
Copyright Renewed
This arrangement Copyright © 2010 INTERIOR MUSIC CORP.
All Rights Controlled and Administered by SONGS OF UNIVERSAL, INC.
All Rights Reserved   Used by Permission

* If melody is out of range, sing notes in parentheses.

Recorded by QUEEN
and Featured in the Twentieth Century Fox Television Series GLEE

SOMEBODY TO LOVE

Original *GLEE* Arrangement
by ADAM ANDERS and TIM DAVIS
Adapted for Publication by TOM ANDERSON

Words and Music by
FREDDIE MERCURY

* If melody is out of range, sing notes in parentheses.

© 1976 (Renewed 2004) QUEEN MUSIC LTD.
This arrangement © 2010 QUEEN MUSIC LTD.
All Rights for the U.S. and Canada Controlled and Administered by BEECHWOOD MUSIC CORP.
All Rights for the world excluding the U.S. and Canada Controlled and Administered by EMI MUSIC PUBLISHING LTD.
All Rights Reserved   International Copyright Secured   Used by Permission

22